Looking after Pip

story by Jenny Alexander

illustrated by Steve Smallman

Pip was crying.
Dad was trying to work.

Dad went to find Jojo and Mouse.
"Can you look after Pip?" he said.

Jojo gave Pip a little cake.
He did not stop crying.

Mouse sang *Old Macdonald had a Farm*.
Pip still did not stop crying.

Jojo played "Boo!" with him.
Even that did not work.

"I know," said Mouse.
"We can take him to the park."

"Good idea!" said Jojo. "Pip loves going to the park."

But Pip did **not** want to go.
He cried all the way there.

Mouse and Jojo saw Grumpyboots down by the pond.

He had his camera.

He was taking a picture of the ducks.

Pip liked the ducks.

He stopped crying.

He waved his cake at them.

The ducks liked Pip's cake.

"Hey!" said Grumpyboots.

"Where have all the ducks gone?"

Grumpyboots looked angry.

"You have spoiled a good picture!" he said.

Mouse wanted to
run away, but it
was too late.
Grumpyboots was
coming towards them.

Then suddenly Grumpyboots stopped.

He smiled.

"This is an even better picture," he said.

Old Grumpyboots got his camera.
"Say quack!" he said
"Quack," they said.

Old Grumpyboots took two pictures.
He gave one of them to Jojo and Mouse.

Jojo and Mouse took Pip home.

Dad was still working.

"We have got a present for you," they said.

They gave him the picture.

He smiled.

"What a good present!" he said.

Just then, Mum came home from work.
She looked at the picture.

"It's Jojo and me," said Mouse.
"I can see that," said Mum.
"But what were you doing?"

"Looking after Pip!" said Jojo.